ANCIENT GREEK CIVILIZATION

This edition published in 2010 by:

The Rosen Publishing Group, Inc.
29 East 21st Street
New York, NY 10010

Additional end matter copyright © 2010 by The Rosen Publishing Group, Inc.

Cover design by Nelson Sa.

Photo Credits: Cover, pp. 1, 3 © www.istockphoto.com/Toon Possemiers; pp. 9 (bottom right), 12 (center) Bildarchiv Preussischer Kulturbesitz/Art Resource, NY; pp. 21(center left), 28 (top left) Erich Lessing/Art Resource, NY.

Library of Congress Cataloging-in-Publication Data

Kuhtz, Cleo.
Ancient Greek civilization / Cleo Kuhtz and Hazel Mary Martell ; illustrations by Francesca D'Ottavi.
    p. cm.—(Ancient civilizations and their myths and legends)
Includes index.
ISBN-13: 978-1-4042-8033-5 (library binding)
1. Mythology, Greek—Juvenile literature. 2. Greece—Civilization—Juvenile literature. I. Martell, Hazel. II. D'Ottavi, Francesca, ill. III. Title.
BL783.K87 2010
292.1'3—dc22

                                                                    2009012203

Manufactured in the United States of America

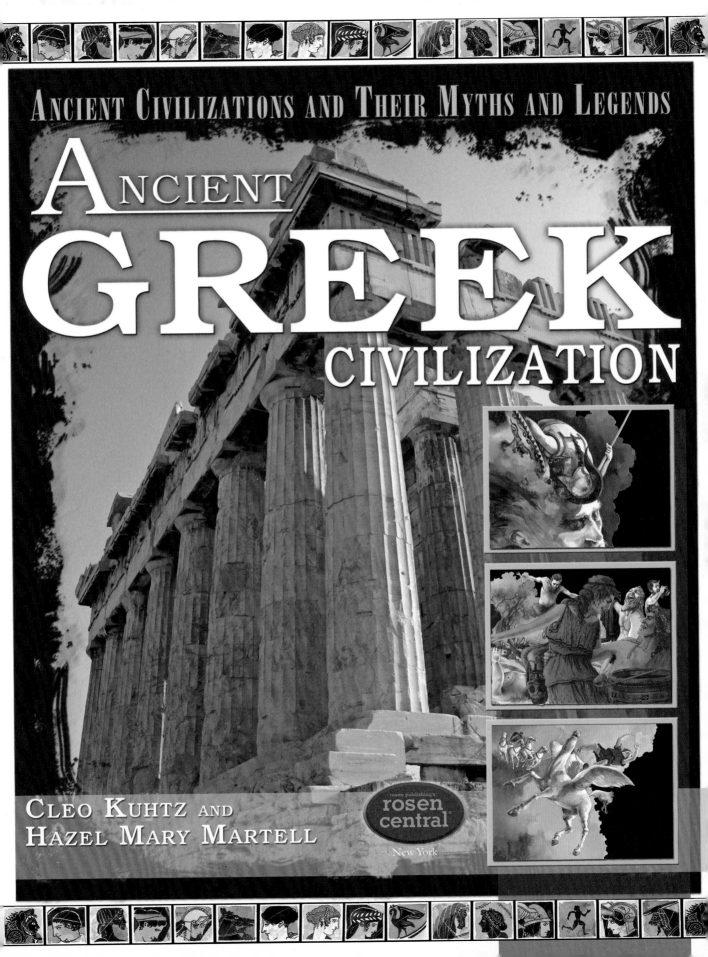

ANCIENT CIVILIZATIONS AND THEIR MYTHS AND LEGENDS

ANCIENT GREEK CIVILIZATION

CLEO KUHTZ AND
HAZEL MARY MARTELL

rosen publishing's
rosen central

New York

CONTENTS

INTRODUCTION 5
How this book works 5

THE BIRTH OF THE GODS 6
Earliest Times 8

CASSANDRA'S GIFT OF PROPHECY 10
Greek Religion 12

THE BIRTH OF ATHENA 14
City-States and Daily Life 16

ARACHNE THE WEAVER 18
Clothes and Jewels 20

DIONYSOS THE SHAPE-CHANGER 22
Entertainment 24

THE SIEGE OF TROY 26
Warfare 28

DAEDALUS AND ICARUS 30
Knowledge and Invention 32

HADES AND PERSEPHONE 34
Agriculture 36

POSEIDON AND PEGASUS 38
Transport and Trade 40

Greek Colonies 42

Glossary 44
For More Information 45
For Further Reading 46
Index 47

INTRODUCTION

The ancient Greeks left us a very rich legacy of stories inspired by their gods, goddesses and heroes. These myths were adopted by the ancient Romans who displaced the Greeks in power in the Mediterranean world. These stories and the Greeks' civilization have been admired and retold ever since and have had a profound influence on the formation of Western culture. It is hard to imagine what European poetry or theater would be like if the Greeks had never existed. Would the explosion of art and learning from the 14th to 16th centuries, which we now call the Renaissance, have taken place if all traces of Greek civilization had vanished? The Greeks also invented democracy and the modern alphabet, and laid the foundations of mathematics, philosophy, astronomy and medicine. This book shows how the mythology and civilization of this influential ancient people were intertwined.

HOW THIS BOOK WORKS

The book is divided into sections. Each one starts with a Greek myth strikingly illustrated on a black background. This is followed by a nonfiction spread with information about an aspect of Greek civilization. The final spread is a nonfiction one explaining how the Greeks set up overseas colonies.

Spread with myth about the siege of Troy leads into a nonfiction spread about warfare.

At its height, the Classical Greek world stretched from southern Italy eastward to the shores of Anatolia (modern Turkey), north around the Black Sea, and south to northern Africa. Each city-state and colony in this vast area had its own religious festivals, myths and legendary heroes. At the same time, they all had a certain number of gods, goddesses and festivals in common. For example, Homer's epic poems, the Iliad and the Odyssey, were known throughout the Greek world and Zeus was the chief god, even if there were local variations in the myths about him.

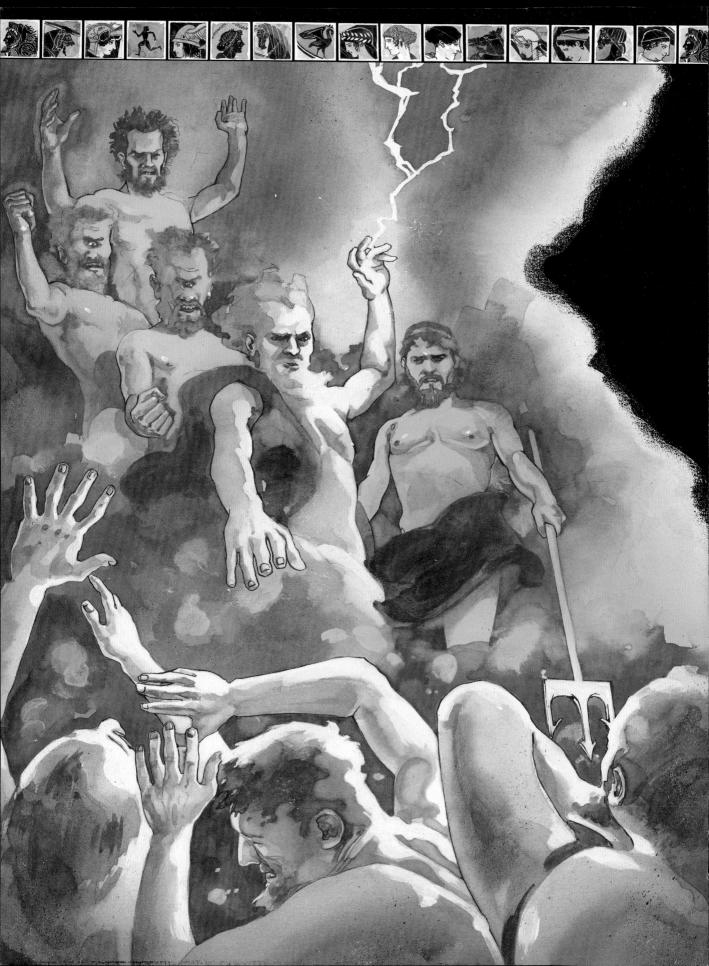

THE BIRTH OF THE GODS

The ancient Greeks believed that, before the gods were born, the universe was in a state of chaos. Gaia, or Earth, emerged from this chaos and gave birth to a son called Uranos, or Sky. She then married him and they had many children. The first to be born were monsters and giants, including the three Cyclopes who only had one eye each, but Uranos banished them from Earth because they were so ugly. Gaia then gave birth to seven Titans and seven Titanesses. They were also giants, but shaped like humans.

Angry over the way Uranos had treated their first children, Gaia encouraged the Titans to rebel against him. They were led by Cronos who attacked his father with a sickle and took over his power. During the attack, however, three drops of Uranos's blood fell on the earth and turned into three creatures known as the Furies, while another drop fell into the sea where it turned into the foam from which Aphrodite, goddess of love and beauty, was born. Cronos then married his sister, the Titaness Rhea, and had five children with her. But, because he had been warned that one of his children would overthrow him, Cronos swallowed each child at birth. Not wanting to lose her sixth child in this way, Rhea wrapped a stone in baby clothes and Cronos swallowed that, while the real child, Zeus, was hidden away and brought up by the Nymphs.

When he was old enough to face his father, Zeus put on a disguise and went back to his home. He gave Cronos a magic potion that made him cough up his three daughters, Hestia, Demeter and Hera, and his other two sons, Hades and Poseidon. Unharmed by the experience, Hades and Poseidon then joined forces with Zeus in the struggle against their father. Zeus brought back the Cyclopes that Uranos had banished and they fought with him, while the Titans fought with Cronos.

The battle between the two sides was long and fierce, but eventually Zeus and his followers defeated Cronos and the Titans and banished most of them to the Underworld. Zeus then became king of all the gods, who were known as the Olympian gods because they lived on Mount Olympus. He married his sister Hera, with whom he had several children, but he also had many more children with other goddesses, mortals and even Titanesses. His brother Poseidon became the god of the Ocean, while Hades became the god of the Underworld.

Earliest Times

The ancient Greek civilization reached its peak during the 5th and 4th centuries BCE. This time, known as the Classical period, saw the development of democratic government, economic and military success, and intense artistic activity, especially in theater, sculpture, architecture, philosophy and history. But this "Golden Age," as it is sometimes called, did not just suddenly happen. Beginning before 2000 BCE, the brilliant Minoan civilization flourished on the Mediterranean island of Crete. It was followed from around 1450 BCE by the Mycenaean civilization on the Greek mainland. The ancient Greeks inherited many things from these earlier peoples.

A silver coin from the Archaic period (700-500 BCE).

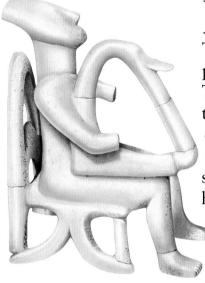

The Cycladic Islands
The Cycladic Islands to the southeast of mainland Greece had one of the earliest civilizations in the Mediterranean. The people made beautiful marble sculptures, like this man playing a harp.

Minoan palaces were decorated with colorful wall paintings. We can learn about Minoan dress and customs by studying them. The painting below comes from the palace at Knossos.

The Minoans
The Minoan civilization, named after its legendary king Minos, was centered on huge palaces from which the kings ruled over the people and organized agriculture and trade. The Minoans had a written language, which archaeologists call Linear A. It has not been deciphered yet. The Mycenaean script, called Linear B, is based on the earlier Minoan one and can be read.

Mycenaean vase dating from 1500 BCE.

The Mycenaeans
During the Mycenaean period Greece was divided into small kingdoms, each of which was ruled from a citadel. The Mycenaeans were influenced by the Minoans and they, in their turn, left much that influenced the ancient Greeks.

The "Dark Ages"

Mycenaean civilization faded around 1250 BCE and a period known as the "Dark Ages" followed during which the knowledge of writing was lost. Little is known of this time, apart from the fact that there were large-scale migrations of people all over the eastern Mediterranean. By about 1000 BCE the ancestors of the ancient Greeks had settled in Greece. Gradually the population began to grow again and cities were rebuilt.

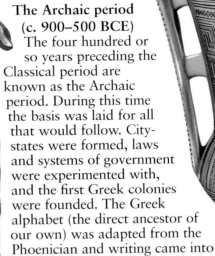

Clay centaur from Lefkandi in central Greece dating from the "Dark Ages."

The Archaic period (c. 900–500 BCE)

The four hundred or so years preceding the Classical period are known as the Archaic period. During this time the basis was laid for all that would follow. City-states were formed, laws and systems of government were experimented with, and the first Greek colonies were founded. The Greek alphabet (the direct ancestor of our own) was adapted from the Phoenician and writing came into use again. There are many sculptures from this time; they are more rigid than the Classical ones, but equally lovely.

Athenian jug with geometric decorations typical of the 8th century BCE.

Very early Classical statue showing Zeus carrying Ganymede off to be his cup-bearer on Mount Olympus. The slight stiffness of the figures is the last legacy of the Archaic period.

The Greek achievement

The ancient Greek civilization is often called the "cradle of the Western World" because so much of what the Greeks achieved is still with us today. The concept of democratic government, ideas about beauty and art, many philosophical and scientific ideas, and the Olympic Games are just four obvious examples. There are many more. Perhaps the Greeks' greatest achievement lay in their ability to think both clearly and creatively.

Late Classical statue showing a mourning girl. Sculptures from this time are realistic, fluid and often express strong sentiments.

Cassandra's Gift of Prophecy

Cassandra was one of the daughters of King Priam of Troy and his wife, Hecuba. Her brother was Paris, whose kidnapping of Helen, the beautiful wife of the Spartan king Menelaus, led to the outbreak of war between Greece and Troy. Cassandra herself was so beautiful that the god Apollo fell in love with her, even though she was a human and not a goddess. He offered her the gift of prophecy in exchange for the promise to marry him. Cassandra accepted Apollo's gift, but then went back on her promise and refused to have anything more to do with him. Angry and disappointed with her, he decided to turn the gift into a curse. Although Cassandra would still be able to predict the future, no one would believe what she said.

Her most important prediction was made while the Greeks were besieging the city of Troy. When the Greeks sent in a large wooden horse as a gift, Cassandra could see that it was a trick that would lead to the downfall of the city. She tried to warn the Trojans, but, as a result of Apollo's curse, not one of them believed her. Their city was overwhelmed and Cassandra herself was taken prisoner by Agamemnon, who was the king of Mycenae and the brother of Menelaus. He was also the husband of Helen's sister, Clytemnestra, but she had been forced to marry him against her will.

Cassandra became Agamemnon's slave and bore him twin sons before returning to Mycenae with him. On the journey to his home, she told Agamemnon that Clytemnestra was planning to murder him. But once more she was not believed and, as Clytemnestra gave Agamemnon a warm welcome and prepared a bath for him, it seemed that Cassandra was wrong. While her husband had been away, however, Clytemnestra had found a lover, Aegisthus, and together they had set a trap for Agamemnon. As he climbed out of the bath, Clytemnestra pretended to be handing him a towel, but in reality she had a net in her hands and threw it over him so that he could not move. Aegisthus then came into the room and stabbed Agamemnon to death, while Clytemnestra killed Cassandra and her two baby sons.

Greek Religion

There were many gods and goddesses in the Greek pantheon. Zeus was the chief god; the others were his brothers, sisters and children. They were believed to rule from a large palace on Mount Olympus. The Greeks worshipped their gods actively and almost every aspect of daily life had some religious meaning or ritual attached to it. Each city-state was dedicated to a god or goddess for whom temples and statues were built and local festivals held. There were many religious festivals and feast days. In Athens, the two most important were the Panathenaia (All-Athens Festival), to celebrate Athena's birthday, and the City Dionysia, in honor of Dionysos.

Relief statue of the goddess Athena in a thoughtful mood. Athena was goddess of Athens and also of knowledge and war. The owl and the olive tree are commonly associated with her.

This statue shows Aphrodite, the goddess of love and beauty.

This powerful statue shows Poseidon. Found by divers in 1928, it was probably stolen by the Romans from a temple dedicated to the god, but lost when their boat sank at sea.

GODS AND GODDESSES

Zeus was the supreme god. He was the god of the sky, storms and thunder, and master of destinies. Demeter was the goddess of agriculture; she was celebrated at festivals in spring and autumn. Apollo was the powerful god of oracles. Apollo's sister, Artemis, was the goddess of initiation, death and the moon. Aphrodite, born from the sea, was the goddess of love. Poseidon was the god of earthquakes, horses and the sea. Nimble Hermes was the gods' messenger as well as the god of shepherds. He also accompanied souls to the Underworld. Dionysos was god of wine and Hestia was the goddess of the home.

1

Oracles

An oracle is the reply a god makes to a question and also the place where this takes place. Most Greeks consulted an oracle before making any important decision, such as who to marry. State decisions, such as where to found a new colony or whether to go to war, were also made after consulting an oracle. The oracle was usually given by priestesses who interpreted the god's reply. The Greeks also believed that special individuals could foresee the future and there were wandering oracle-sellers and fortune-tellers who made a living this way.

Most of the important gods were worshipped all over Greece. Many had sanctuaries dedicated to them in various parts of the Greek world. This map shows some of the largest sanctuaries.

The Oracle of Apollo was the oldest and most important oracle in the ancient world. This painting shows a man asking a question of one of the priestesses at the oracle.

The Parthenon, the main temple on the acropolis of Athens, was dedicated to Athena.

Dodona *Zeus*
Ege *Poseidon*
Delphi *Apollo*
Corinth *Poseidon*
Mycenae *Hera*
Eleusis *Demeter*
Athens *Athena*
Halicarnassus
Olympia *Zeus*
Epidaurus *Asklepios* *Poseidon*
Sparta *Artemis, Hera*
Rhodes *Aphrodite*

*Scenes from a workshop:
1 Craftsman finishing a statue that has already been cast; only the head is missing. 2 A bronze is smelted in a furnace. 3 Finishing a statue involved sanding and polishing the surface.*

Building for the gods

The Greeks built temples and sanctuaries and dedicated them to their gods. They were usually decorated with statues of gods and goddesses. Skilled craftspeople were employed to make these. This relief carving shows the various stages involved in casting and carving a statue.

THE BIRTH OF ATHENA

The goddess Athena was the daughter of Zeus and Metis, who was the Titaness of wisdom. But, before Athena was born, Zeus was told that any son born to Metis would grow up to be more important than his father. Not knowing whether the child that Metis was expecting would be a girl or a boy, Zeus decided to solve the problem by changing Metis into a fly and swallowing her. Shortly afterward, however, while he was out walking with Hephaestos, the blacksmith to the gods, Zeus began to suffer from a terrible headache. He told Hephaestos to hit him on the head to relieve the pain. Hephaestos obeyed and for a moment Zeus's skull cracked open and out stepped the adult Athena, dressed in armor and ready for battle.

She carried a spear and a shield and wore a helmet, but because she had inherited wisdom from her mother, her symbol was the owl. This wisdom led her to try to solve arguments by reasoning, rather than by fighting, though the people she supported in warfare always won their battles.

One of Athena's own greatest arguments was with Poseidon, the sea god, as she wanted the most important town in Greece to be named after her, while he wanted it to be named after him. The people of the town suggested that Athena and Poseidon each make a practical gift to the town and the inhabitants would then name the town after whoever had come up with the most useful idea.

The town was built around a rock known as the Acropolis. Poseidon hit it with his trident and a stream started to pour out, quickly giving access from the town to the sea. Then Athena touched the same rock with her spear and the first olive tree sprang out of the ground. As well as providing food, its fruits could be crushed to make oil for lighting and cooking. The townspeople realized that this was not only useful for them, but could also be exported in exchange for gold, silver or other goods. This made them decide that Athena's was the better gift and so they named their town Athens after her. A shrine known as the Parthenon was built for her on top of the Acropolis and Athena then became their special goddess and guardian of their town.

City-States and Daily Life

One of the most distinctive features of ancient Greece was the way it was divided into many small, independent states, called "city-states." By around 700 BCE almost all of Greece was divided up in this way. Gradually most city-states developed some form of democratic government. This meant that adult male citizens (women, children, foreigners and slaves were excluded) voted to elect representatives who governed on their behalf. The elected governors met in the *agora* (marketplace) where they discussed and then voted on how their city-state should be run. The agora was also the market and meeting place for all the inhabitants of the city-state.

The owl, symbol of the goddess Athena, was also a symbol of Athens, the city named in her honor.

Unpopular citizens or political rivals could be sent into exile by the other citizens. A vote was held, and if the majority were in favor, the unwanted citizen was sent away for up to ten years. His name was scratched into broken pottery.

Acropolis
Temple
Agora
River
City walls
Port

The structure of city-states

Each of the several hundred city-states in ancient Greece was composed of a town (usually enclosed by walls for protection) and the surrounding countryside. The towns all had an acropolis on a hill or raised ground with a temple dedicated to the god or goddess of the town, as well as an agora where people could meet. Almost all the city-states were situated on the coast or on a river to allow easy access for merchant ships and warships.

Athens was one of the most democratic of the city-states. This vase painting shows the citizens of Athens voting.

Slaves

Slavery was common in ancient Greece and almost all families owned at least one to do the heavy household chores. A really rich person might own as many as fifty.

Athenian statesman Pericles was a superb orator (public speaker) and a great politician. He led Athens at her time of greatest glory in the 440s and 430s BCE.

Athens

Athens was one of the largest, wealthiest and most powerful city-states. During the Classical period it became the intellectual and cultural center of the Greek world. The focus of daily life centered on the agora (marketplace), while the city itself was dominated by the newly rebuilt temples on the Acropolis. Although Athens was beaten by Sparta in 404 BCE, it remained important and influential for several centuries.

This vase painting shows a slave.

Trades and crafts

The agora and surrounding streets were filled with craftspeople and traders making and selling their wares. Butchers, bakers, cobblers, potters, barbers, money-changers and many others were all crowded in together.

Family life

Ancient Greek families were usually made up of a married couple and their children. If they were reasonably wealthy, their house would have a separate *gynaeceum* (women's quarters) where the female members of the family spent most of their time. Women lived very secluded lives and were not allowed to go out of the house without good reason. Women from poorer families went out to work, so they probably had a little more freedom. Men of all walks of life spent most of their time away from home. Farmers tended their fields, craftspeople and traders worked in the town, while wealthy men gathered together to discuss town government and to gossip.

Woman putting household goods away in a cabinet. Furniture was simple and light, and most homes just had a few basic pieces.

ARACHNE THE WEAVER

In ancient Greece most women knew how to spin wool into yarn and cloth, but not one of them was as skilled as the princess Arachne. She could take the finest thread and weave it into the most delicate cloth. Unfortunately, she was rather conceited and liked to boast about her skills. One day she even boasted that she could weave better than Athena who was the goddess of home crafts, as well as being the goddess of wisdom and war.

Athena was also proud of her weaving skills and, when she heard of Arachne's boast, she challenged the princess to a weaving contest. Arachne accepted the challenge and she and Athena set up their looms. Neither the goddess nor the princess looked at each other as they wove their cloth. Instead, they both concentrated on doing their very best work. The goddess thought she would win easily and at the same time teach Arachne not to be so boastful in the future. When they had finished, however, Athena was horrified to realize that the length of cloth that Arachne had woven was every bit as beautiful as the one she had woven herself. Overcome with jealousy and anger, she ripped Arachne's cloth from the loom and tore it into shreds.

Arachne was terrified by Athena's anger and, realizing that the goddess would never forgive her, she ran from the room and hanged herself from a tree. Athena chased after her, but when she saw what Arachne had done, the goddess's anger melted away and she felt ashamed of herself for behaving so badly. Taking pity on Arachne, Athena decided to bring her back to life again so that her weaving skills would not be lost. But the goddess still could not bear the thought of any mortal being a better weaver than she was and so, rather than make Arachne human again, Athena turned her rival into a spider who would spend the rest of her life spinning fine thread and weaving it into beautiful webs.

Making cloth

Greek women made all the woolen cloth they needed for clothes and other items. They started with a sheep's fleece that had to be washed and dyed. The wool was then spun by hand into yarn and woven into cloth on an upright loom.

Detail from a vase painting showing Penelope sitting sadly beside her loom as she waits for her husband Odysseus to return from the wars.

Gold earring in the shape of a boat. It was made in the 4th century BCE.

Clothes and Jewels

Ancient Greek men and women wore simple tunics, made from fine wool or linen. Known as *chitons*, they were made from two rectangles of cloth sewn together down the sides. They were often gathered at the waist with a belt or girdle so that they fell in soft pleats. Women and older men wore their chitons to their ankles, but younger men wore shorter chitons or pulled them up over their belts to make it easier to move around.

Indoors people went barefoot, but when they went outside they wore leather sandals in the summer and shoes or boots in the winter, when they also wore thick cloaks, called *himations*, to keep themselves warm.

Jewelry for the rich

Wealthy Greek women often wore ornate jewelry made from gold or silver. As well as wearing pendants, bracelets, rings and brooches, they had their ears pierced for earrings. On special occasions, they sometimes also wore delicate gold or silver ornaments in their hair.

Men's clothes

Not all Greek men wore a tunic. Younger ones often just wore a *himation*, while slaves and craftworkers wore a simple loincloth. When they were outside in summer, however, most men wore large-brimmed hats to protect themselves from the sun. They also sometimes wore a shorter cloak, called a *chlamys*, which was fastened on the shoulder with a pin.

Men's hairstyles

At first Greek men wore their hair long and also had full beards and moustaches. Later, shorter hair and beards became more fashionable, while the last of the ancient Greeks were clean-shaven. Statues tell us a great deal about fashions in hairstyles.

Head of the Rampin Horseman, *showing an elaborate hairstyle from the Archaic period.*

Women's clothes

Although women's clothes were simple, they were often dyed in bright colors and had contrasting borders. Many of the dyes were obtained from plants, but others were made from sea snails and insect larvae.

This detail from a cup shows a woman holding a mirror next to a washbasin.

The backs of mirrors were often highly decorated.

In the Archaic period women wore their hair long.

Hygiene

Cleanliness was important to the Greeks, and both rich and poor washed and bathed frequently. Rich people had small terra-cotta baths in their houses, while poor people washed in large pots, often filled with water from the nearest public fountain. After a bath many people rubbed perfumed oil into their skin to stop it drying out.

Cosmetics and perfume

Many Greek women wore make-up. They often darkened their eyebrows and used rouge to make their cheeks pink. Pale skin was fashionable and so they also used cosmetics to make their faces as white as possible. After they had washed their hair they put perfumed oil on it to make it shine. Wearing perfume on the skin was also fashionable.

Changing fashions

Fashion changed very slowly in ancient Greece, but in the 5th and 4th centuries BCE two new materials—cotton and silk—became available. But only the rich could afford to have their clothes made from them.

DIONYSOS THE SHAPE-CHANGER

Dionysos was both the god of wine and the god of the theater. His father was the god Zeus and his mother was Semele, the daughter of the king of Thebes. When she was expecting a child, Semele was tricked by Zeus's jealous wife Hera into asking Zeus to reveal himself to her in all his glory. Knowing that seeing him in this state would mean instant death for Semele because she was a mortal, Zeus was reluctant to agree to her request, but eventually he was persuaded to appear in his heavenly chariot, surrounded by thunderbolts and lightning. Semele took one look and was turned to ashes, but Zeus saved the child she was expecting and it became Dionysos.

As Dionysos grew up, he was cared for by Silenus, one of the less important gods who spent most of his time on earth. Silenus enjoyed life to the fullest, however, and often acted irresponsibly.

He liked to get drunk and his companions, known as the Satyrs, enjoyed chasing girls. Together with Dionysos, they traveled around the world, having a good time and spreading the knowledge of making wine from grapes. They often annoyed people, however, and Dionysos sometimes had to get out of trouble by changing from human form into an animal.

On one of his adventures, Dionysos hired a ship to take him from the port of Icaria to the island of Naxos. But, unknown to him, the ship belonged to pirates and, once they had him on board,

they planned to take him to a foreign country and sell him as a slave. To prevent his escape, they tried to tie him up with a rope, but the knots would not stay fastened. Then Dionysos used his powers to turn their oars into snakes and make vines and ivy grow around the masts of the ship so that the sails could not be hoisted. When the pirates still refused to release him, he turned himself into a ferocious lion and chased them around the ship until they all jumped into the sea. There they were turned into dolphins, while Dionysos returned to his normal shape and continued his journey.

Entertainment

Wealthy Greeks had slaves and servants to carry out most of the hard work and daily chores. This left them with plenty of spare time to enjoy sporting events, the theater, banquets, festivals and feast days, music, games and, perhaps the most common pastime of all, conversation. Although rich women were excluded from many of the public events, they held ladies' parties and met together in the women's quarters to chat and exchange news.

Sculpted portrait of the great Athenian playwright, Sophocles.

A Greek actor, dressed ready for his entry and holding his mask. Actors wore masks throughout each performance.

Stage

Orchestra

Greek plays were performed in steep-sided, open-air theaters. The two or three main actors were accompanied by a chorus who sang, danced and commented on the proceedings from the orchestra.

Theater

Greek theater reached its peak in Athens during the Classical period. A four-day-long drama festival was held each spring during which the Athenians chose the best play. This and other performances encouraged dramatists such as Aeschylus, Sophocles, Euripides, Menander and Aristophanes to write their masterpieces.

Sport

Sport was very important to the Greeks and good athletes were regarded with respect. All Greek boys trained hard from an early age. The main sports were running, long-jump, wrestling, javelin and discus throwing. The first Olympic Games were held at Olympia in 776 BCE.

Few women were allowed to take part in sporting events. However, girls in some religious sanctuaries ran, and Spartan women are thought to have competed in athletic contests.

This famous statue, called the Discus Thrower, is a Roman copy of a Greek statue.

Bards and Storytelling

In Archaic times bards recited stories and poems with music to entertain and keep people informed. The poet Homer, who composed the famous epic poems the *Iliad* and the *Odyssey*, was probably a bard.

An 8th-century BCE statue found on Crete shows a bard playing a lyre.

Banquets

Greek men often held banqueting parties. Respectable women were excluded from these parties, although slave women were often present to dance and entertain the guests. The men reclined comfortably on couches as they ate, drank and talked far into the night.

Bronze statue of a banqueter reclining on a couch, wine cup in hand.

Music

Music was an important part of daily life in Greece. Theater, banquets and religious festivals were all accompanied by music. But so, too, were ordinary events, such as baking bread, and athletic and military training. Common instruments included pipes, lyres, flutes, drums and cymbals.

Greek woman playing reed pipes.

This painted ceramic statue shows two girls playing knucklebones. The knucklebones were made from sheep or cattle vertebrae.

Games and Toys

Greek children had toys and games to keep them occupied. Toys included hoops, rattles, spinning tops and brightly colored statues of animals and people. Board games and knucklebones were played by men, women and children.

THE SIEGE OF TROY

When Paris, the King of Troy's son, abducted Helen, the wife of King Menelaus of Sparta, and refused to return her to her husband, the Greeks declared war on the Trojans. Led by Menelaus's brother, Agamemnon, they gathered a fleet of a thousand ships and set sail for Troy. By the time they got there, however, Helen had enchanted all the Trojans with her beauty and charm and they were prepared to fight the Greeks rather than give her back to them.

Fortunately for the Trojans, Troy had thick walls and strong gates but, although the Greeks besieged the city, their army was not powerful enough to drive the Greeks away. The siege went on for ten years and men were killed on both sides, but neither the Trojans nor the Greeks would give up the fight. Then Odysseus, King of Ithaca and the Greeks' chief warrior, thought of a way to trick the Trojans into letting the Greek army into their city.

Following Odysseus's instructions, the Greeks built a huge wooden horse, but it was hollow, with enough space inside for several armed warriors. The warriors got into the horse and it was placed outside the gates of Troy. All but one of the other Greek warriors then went to their ships and started to sail away. The Trojans saw this and thought the Greeks were giving up. They also saw the horse and the one Greek warrior who had been left behind. He told them that, if they took the horse into Troy, it would protect the city for ever. Paris's sister, Cassandra, tried to warn the Trojans against this, but they would not listen. They pulled the horse through the gates and began to celebrate their victory. When darkness fell and the Trojans went to their beds, the Greek warriors climbed out of their hiding place and quickly opened the gates of Troy to let in the rest of the Greek army that had been waiting just offshore. The Trojans were defeated, their city was ransacked, and Helen was captured and returned to Menelaus.

Warfare

War was a constant feature in Greek civilization. Homer's epic poem, the *Iliad*, which includes the story of the siege of Troy, is thought to be based on historical events dating from the Mycenaean age. Centuries later, the Greek city-states banded together to defend themselves against the Persian Empire. Not long after the Persian threat subsided around 479 BCE, the Peloponnesian Wars broke out. They were fought between the two major city-states, Athens and Sparta, but involved almost all the others as well. The Greek world also produced one of the greatest soldiers ever known. Alexander the Great (356–323 BCE) conquered an enormous empire that stretched 18,641 miles (30,000 kilometers) from Greece to India.

This vase painting shows a soldier saying goodbye to his wife as he leaves for war.

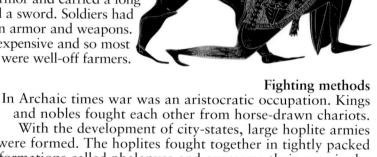

Soldiers

During the 7th century BCE the Greeks developed a suit of armor and a specialized way of fighting. Hoplites (foot soldiers) were the basic unit in Greek armies. Each soldier wore armor and carried a long spear, a shield and a sword. Soldiers had to buy their own armor and weapons. This was quite expensive and so most hoplites were well-off farmers.

Fighting methods

In Archaic times war was an aristocratic occupation. Kings and nobles fought each other from horse-drawn chariots. With the development of city-states, large hoplite armies were formed. The hoplites fought together in tightly packed formations called phalanxes and overcame their enemies by strength of numbers rather than individual skill.

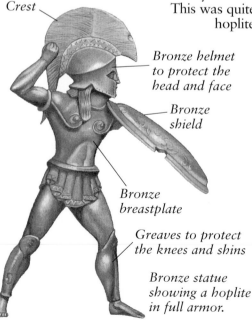

Crest

Bronze helmet to protect the head and face

Bronze shield

Bronze breastplate

Greaves to protect the knees and shins

Bronze statue showing a hoplite in full armor.

Soldiers in a phalanx marched with their spears extended. As soldiers in the front row fell, they were quickly replaced by the men behind them and the group acted like a battering ram.

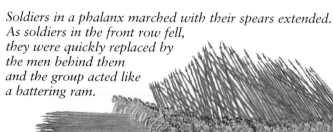

Greek warships

The Greeks were skilled sailors, probably because the mountainous land they inhabited made sea travel more practical than overland routes. Many city-states formed large navies. In the early 4th century BCE the Athenian fleet consisted of over 400 triremes. There were only a few soldiers on each ship and naval battles were won by ramming the enemy's ships at high speed rather than by combat between soldiers.

The earliest Greek warships were penteconters. They were single-level galleys rowed by fifty oarsmen (twenty-five per side).

The lighter and faster bireme came into use in the 7th century BCE. It was rowed by fifty-six oarsmen, seated on two levels. It was widely used for about three centuries.

The trireme was manned by 170 oarsmen seated on three levels. It became the classic Greek warship and was still used by the Romans centuries after it first appeared in Corinth around 700 BCE.

Statue of a Spartan warrior. Spartan men spent their entire lives as soldiers. They were taken from their families to begin training when they were seven years old.

Detail from a mosaic showing Alexander the Great at the Battle of Issus (333 BCE), where he defeated Darius, the Persian king.

Alexander the Great

Alexander was only twenty years old when he became king of Macedonia. When he died just twelve years later, he had conquered the largest empire the world had ever known. Alexander was a great soldier (he led his men into battle himself, rather than watching from the sidelines) and an able politician. As he moved his huge army eastward toward India, he spread Greek language, culture and thought across the region.

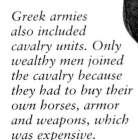

Greek armies also included cavalry units. Only wealthy men joined the cavalry because they had to buy their own horses, armor and weapons, which was expensive.

DAEDALUS AND ICARUS

Daedalus was a skilled craftsman and inventor who lived in ancient Athens. He was a member of the royal household and had a son called Icarus. He had a nephew called Perdix who was also an inventor. When Perdix claimed to have invented the saw, however, Daedalus was overcome with jealousy. He killed Perdix by throwing him over a cliff, then fled into exile on the island of Crete, taking Icarus with him.

Crete at that time was ruled by King Minos. He had asked Poseidon, god of the sea, to give him a bull that he would then sacrifice to the god. But when the bull arrived, it was so magnificent that Minos did not want to kill it. Instead he tried to sacrifice another bull in its place. This angered Poseidon so much that, for revenge, he made Minos's wife, Pasiphae, fall in love with the bull. Taking pity on her, Daedalus helped Pasiphae to meet the bull by building a beautiful, life-size model of a cow with enough room inside for her to hide. As a result of this meeting, however, Pasiphae gave birth to the Minotaur, a fierce creature that was half-human and half-bull.

As the Minotaur grew up, it became fond of eating human flesh and terrorizing people, so Minos instructed Daedalus to do something to keep it under control. So Daedalus built a complicated maze, known as the Labyrinth. Once it was put in the middle of the Labyrinth, the Minotaur could not find a way out and had to stay there for the rest of its life.

Then Daedalus fell out of favor with Minos and ended up in prison himself. Icarus was with him and, realizing that Minos would kill them both, Daedalus thought up a way of escape. Using wax and feathers, he made a pair of wings for Icarus and another for himself and together they flew out of the window.

Daedalus warned Icarus not to go too near to the sun because of the wax in his wings, but once he was in the air, Icarus found that he liked flying so much that he forgot his father's warning. He flew higher and higher, until suddenly the wax melted and his wings fell apart. Icarus plunged into the sea and was drowned, leaving Daedalus to fly on alone to a new life on the island of Sicily.

Knowledge and Invention

Greek mathematicians, scientists and philosophers made an enormous contribution to knowledge and learning in the Western world. Many of their discoveries and theories are still in use today. Some Greek ideas were far ahead of their time. For example, Aristarchus of Samos, a Greek astronomer who lived in the 3rd century BCE, was the first to realize that the earth rotates on itself once every twenty-four hours and that the earth and other planets revolve around the sun. His theory was ignored for 1700 years until Copernicus proved him right in the 16th century CE.

Bust of the philosopher and mathematician Pythagoras.

Teacher and pupil from a painting on a Greek vase.

The alphabet

When the Mycenaean civilization declined during the 12th century BCE, the knowledge of writing disappeared, too. Four hundred years later the ancient Greeks invented an entirely new system of writing. Its use spread very quickly. The alphabet used by the ancient Greeks is still used in Greece today. Many writing systems, including our own Latin alphabet, are based on the Greek one.

Education

Boys from wealthy families went to school from the age of seven. They had to be wealthy because schools were all private and parents had to pay for their children's educations. At school the boys learned reading, writing and arithmetic. They also learned to play a musical instrument and to recite poetry. Girls did not go to school. They stayed at home with their mothers and learned how to run a home. Some women did learn to read and write because they were taught by male members of the family.

The twenty-four letters of the Greek alphabet with their Latin equivalents.

alpha	A	a
beta	B	b
gamma	Γ	g
delta	Δ	d
epsilon	E	e
zeta	Z	z
eta	H	e
theta	Θ	th
iota	I	i
kappa	K	c, k
lambda	Λ	l
mu	M	m
nu	N	n
xi	Ξ	x
omicron	O	o
pi	Π	p
rho	P	r, rh
sigma	Σ	s
tau	T	t
upsilon	Y	y, u
phi	Φ	ph
chi	X	ch
psi	Ψ	ps
omega	Ω	o

Medicine

The Greeks were among the first people to think of illness and disease as natural occurrences that should be treated scientifically rather than by using magic or religious cures. They developed a core of basic knowledge that could be handed down. During Hellenistic times they studied anatomy and even used surgery to treat patients.

Philosophy

Thales of Miletus, a Greek philosopher who lived in the 6th century BCE, introduced a system of reasoned thinking and explanation of the world that is still valid today. The teachings of other Greek philosophers, such as Socrates, Plato and Aristotle, laid the basis for philosophy in the Western world.

Stone portrait head of a philosopher from Hellenistic times.

This stone relief carving shows a doctor as he works on a patient. During the 5th century BCE the writings of a scientist called Hippocrates were collected. Doctors in many countries today still swear a "Hippocratic oath" at the start of their careers. The oath is a kind of ethical code of conduct for doctors.

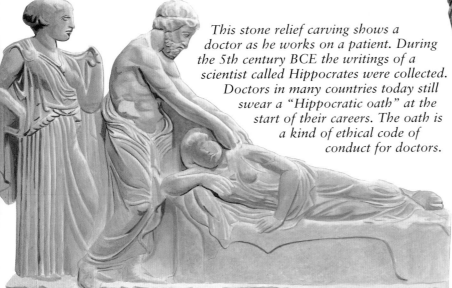

The ancient Greeks used the abacus for mathematical and business calculations.

Greek scientists designed many amazing inventions, although most were never built. The diagram shows a model of Hero of Alexandria's aeolipile—the first known steam-powered engine.

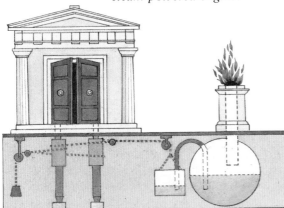

Mathematics

The Greeks can be considered the inventors of modern mathematics because they made it a theoretical science, in which all statements have to be general and they all need to be proved.

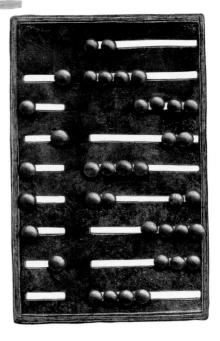

HADES AND PERSEPHONE

Hades was the god of the Underworld. He was very rich but very lonely because nobody wanted to live in his dark and gloomy kingdom. Sometimes he visited the earth just to look at the people there. On one of his visits he saw Persephone gathering flowers in a field and fell in love with her. She was the daughter of Demeter, the goddess of plants and harvests. The two of them were very close and Persephone often helped Demeter in her work.

Realizing that Demeter would never give him permission to marry Persephone, Hades decided to abduct her. He grabbed her by the hair and pushed her into his chariot, then raced back to the Underworld with her. Not knowing where her daughter had gone, Demeter neglected the earth and set out to look for her. The flowers withered and the leaves fell from the trees. The crops stopped growing and the people started to go hungry. Then, when she found out what had happened to Persephone, Demeter asked Zeus to help her. He told her that Persephone could return to the earth, providing she had not eaten anything while she was in the Underworld, and he sent Hermes the messenger to command Hades to set her free.

Meanwhile Persephone had been refusing to eat. But when Hades offered her twelve juicy seeds from a pomegranate, she found she was too hungry to resist. When Hermes arrived, she had already eaten six of them. Hades said that meant she would have to stay with him forever, but Zeus intervened. He said that because Persephone had only eaten six seeds, she only had to spend six months of every year in the Underworld. For the other six months she could return to the earth and be with her mother. Demeter agreed and, while Persephone was with her, she tended the plants and made them grow. When her daughter had to go back to the Underworld, however, Demeter let all the plants wither and die and did not tend them again until Persephone came back to her.

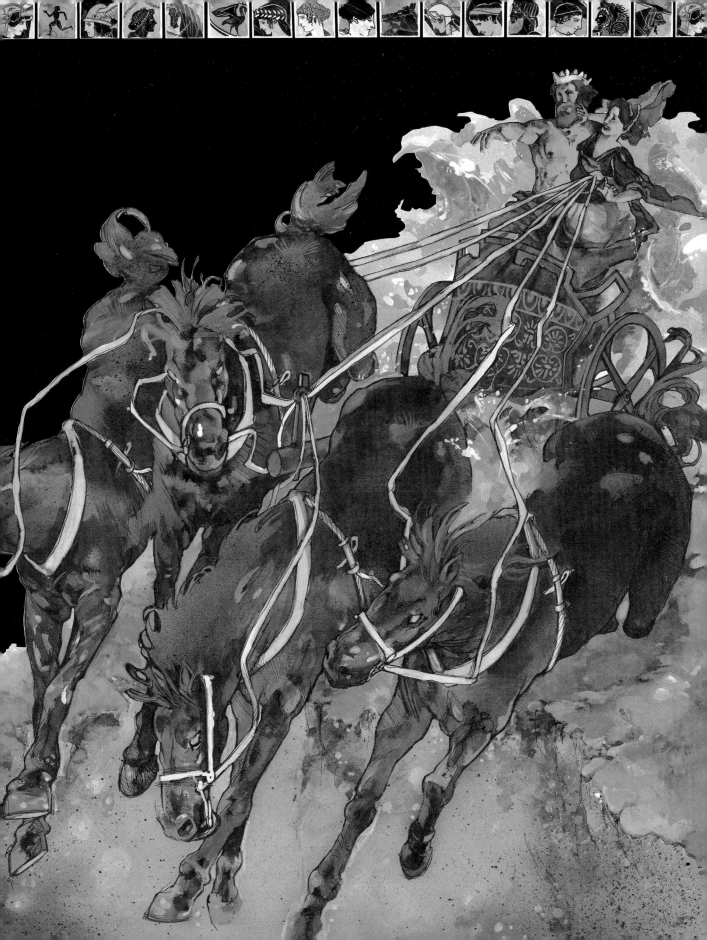

Agriculture

The people of ancient Greece grew the food they needed on small farms scattered throughout the countryside. Farming was not easy, however, because the land was arid and hilly and the climate could be harsh, especially in summer when little rain fell. The farmers overcame these difficulties by using the most fertile soil for their grain crops and planting vineyards on the lower slopes of the hills. Olive trees, however, would grow on high ground or poor soil, which could also be used for grazing sheep and goats. Small fields around the farmhouse were used for growing fruit, such as apples, pears and figs, and vegetables, such as cabbage, lentils and onions. Bees were also kept to provide honey for sweetening things.

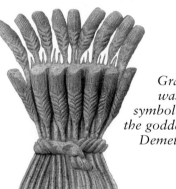

A small votive statue of a man carrying a sheep.

Cattle and oxen
Cattle were raised for their milk, rather than for meat, in areas where there was good grazing. Most farmers also kept a couple of oxen that they used to pull the plow over fields in autumn.

Harvesting olives
Olives were one of the most important crops on the farm. Some were eaten as part of a meal, but most were crushed to produce oil. This was used for cooking and for lighting and as the basis of many beauty products.

Help from the gods
Farmers often left small statues like this one at a shrine or temple when they wanted the gods to give them good harvests and healthy animals.

Greek coins from grape-growing areas were often decorated with bunches of grapes.

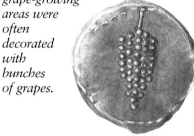

Vase painting showing people with long sticks knocking ripe olives out of the trees.

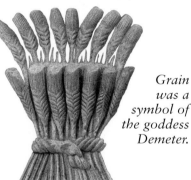

Grain was a symbol of the goddess Demeter.

Growing grapes
Grapes grew well in all parts of Greece. When they were harvested in September, some were dried in the sun to be eaten later as raisins, but most were trodden or pressed and made into wine.

The importance of grain
Barley and wheat were grown in ancient Greece, but barley was the most common. Its grain was ground into flour that was for making bread and a thick porridge that was eaten with vegetables for the evening meal.

This detail from a vase painting shows Greek farmers plowing and sowing crops.

The farming year

Greek farmers worked to the same pattern each year, plowing the fields and planting barley or wheat seeds in October. These grew through the winter when most rain fell and the crop was harvested in April or May. The field was then left unplanted to let fertility return to the soil, before the cycle began again in October.

Life on the farm

Farmhouses were simple buildings made from mud bricks covered in plaster and roofed with clay tiles. The small windows were set high up in the walls for privacy and security. Near the house were the olive press and the grape press, shelters for the animals and storage places for grain, olive oil and fermenting wine.

Olives were harvested in late autumn. The oil was pressed out of the fruit using a hand-operated press, like the one shown here.

Farm animals

Shepherds looked after the sheep and goats when they were grazing on the hills. They provided wool and meat, and skins that could be made into leather. The ewes gave milk that was made into cheese. Pigs and poultry were also kept for their meat.

POSEIDON AND PEGASUS

Poseidon was the god of the sea and the brother of Zeus and Hades. He had control over all the sea monsters and could calm storms by riding over the sea in his golden chariot that was pulled by a team of white horses. He could also cause earthquakes by striking the ground with his trident. His many offspring included giants and monsters, as well as mortals and the winged horse, Pegasus.

The mother of Pegasus was Medusa, one of the Gorgons. She met Poseidon in one of Athena's temples. This angered Athena so much that she turned Medusa's hair into snakes and made her and her two sisters into monsters who would turn into stone any mortal who looked at their faces. Later, Athena helped Perseus, the mortal son of Zeus and Danae, to kill Medusa by giving him a polished shield in which he could see Medusa's reflection while keeping his back turned to her. Athena also gave Perseus a crystal sword with which he could cut off Medusa's head. When he did this, Medusa's blood spilled on the ground and Pegasus sprang out of it.

Unlike his mother, Pegasus was good-natured and obedient, doing as he was told by either Athena or Poseidon. When the mortal Bellerophon was sent to kill the fire-breathing monster known as the Chimera, Pegasus was sent to help him. Bellerophon climbed onto his back and Pegasus flew with him far enough from the Chimera for its fire not to burn them, but close enough for Bellerophon to plunge his spear down the Chimera's throat.

Unfortunately, Bellerophon enjoyed flying on Pegasus so much that he decided to use him to fly to the gods' home on Mount Olympus. As no mortal was allowed to go there without an invitation, Bellerophon's action made the gods very angry. Zeus decided to punish him by sending a fly to bite Pegasus under his tail. Pegasus went wild with the pain and, as he reared up, Bellerophon was thrown from his back and went crashing back to earth. Pegasus himself became one of Zeus's servants and eventually turned into a group of stars shining in the night sky.

Transport and Trade

The geography of Greece—it's barren, hilly mainland and many islands—made overland travel impractical. From the earliest times people traveled and transported goods by sea rather than by road. City-states preferred to invest money in merchant ships than in roads. The few roads that did exist generally led to temples. Worshippers visited the temples on foot, or riding on a donkey or horse. As the city-states grew richer, large fleets of merchant ships were formed and cargoes were carried the length and breadth of the Mediterranean and even farther afield.

Horses or donkeys were used to pull two- or four-wheeled carts. Donkeys were also the main beasts of burden and carried enormous weights in saddlebags tied on each side of their backs.

Greek imports

There was too little fertile land for the Greeks to grow enough wheat and other cereals, so they had to import large quantities from abroad. As the population increased, cereals were brought from areas as far away as southern Russia. The Greek city-states also imported wood, slaves, wool, precious metals, wine, olive oil, salt fish and fish sauce (*garum*), exotic animals and many other items from other city-states, Greek colonies abroad or from foreign countries.

This decorated dish shows the god Dionysos in a sailing boat. He has just been attacked by pirates but has performed a miracle by turning the pirates into dolphins. Piracy was common along the major trade routes and powerful city-states, such as Athens, had a fleet of warships to accompany their merchant ships on dangerous journeys.

Metal coins were first used in Anatolia (modern Turkey) in the 7th century BCE. They soon spread through-out the Greek world. Each city-state minted its own coins.

Olives and olive oil

The Mediterranean climate and soils are perfect for growing olives and olives have been an important food in the region since earliest times. For the ancient Greeks the fruit was even more important for the oil extracted from it. Olive oil was used for cooking, lighting, medicines, perfumes and body oils. It was also used in some religious ceremonies. Oil was one of the principal exports of the Greek city-states.

Greek exports

The agora (marketplace) in Greek towns was usually surrounded by workshops where skilled craftspeople made and sold pottery, jewelry, leather goods, sculptures, engravings and many other items. Anything not bought by local people was sold to merchants for export.

This oil flask in the form of a very expressive owl shows the exquisite taste and decorative skills of Greek craftspeople.

Greek merchant ships were propelled with sails and oars. They came in all shapes and sizes, but judging by some of the wrecks that archaeologists have discovered, many of them must have been very large indeed. Liquid cargoes, such as wine and oil, was stored in amphorae (jars), while grain was packed in sacks. Many merchant ships had deep holds where the goods were stored during the journey.

There was no coffee or tea in ancient Greece and people drank a lot of wine. It was often added to water. Wine was made in many parts of Greece and exported to the cities or abroad.

ATHENS—CENTER OF TRADE

Trade was vital to the economy of Athens. The city had a population of about 500,000 in the 5th century BCE, but the farmland in Attica, the area around Athens, was unsuitable for growing wheat, the staple food. Because of the enormous amount of wheat that had to be imported to feed the people, Athens became a bustling center of trade. The city's port of Piraeus was rebuilt and linked to the city by a walled road. The Athenian government controlled the wheat trade by protecting the major trade routes, prohibiting stockpiling and re-export, and by appointing officials to oversee the market. Shipbuilders, bankers, insurance agents, merchants and dealers of all types benefited from the flourishing wheat trade. Contacts were established with foreign merchants, and many of the luxury items, such as pottery, jewelry and fine cloth, made by the highly skilled craftspeople of Athens were exported far and wide.

This painted dish shows the ruler of a Greek colony in North Africa as he oversees the weighing and storage of herbs.

Greek Colonies

From the 8th century BCE, the Greeks began settling in colonies outside Greece. These outposts were probably originally set up as trading centers, but as the population of the city-states grew they also served as overspill towns to relieve the pressure of population at home. Trade was important for the livelihoods of almost all the colonies. Most of them depended heavily on farming and much of what they produced was shipped back to the homeland. Because sea or river transport was the easiest way of shipping goods over long distances, colonies were usually situated on rivers or where coastlines made good sea ports.

Decorated knee and leg armor from Thrace (Bulgaria). It shows a mixture of Greek and Thracian elements.

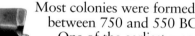

The first colonies

Most colonies were formed between 750 and 550 BCE. One of the earliest was founded around 750 BCE on the coast near Naples (Italy). The Greeks wanted the iron that was mined on the island of Elba to the north, but they did not dare settle there because the Etruscans from central Italy controlled the island. Most Greek colonies were in the eastern Mediterranean because in the west they had rivals such as the Etruscans and Carthaginians.

The Black Sea colonies

The Greeks originally settled the shores of the Black Sea because it gave them access to the wheat-growing lands of southern Russia. Over the years Greek culture mixed with the local one; archaeologists have found artifacts that combine elements of both cultures.

Love of adventure

The civilization of ancient Greece is marked by the people's willingness to explore everything, from a new idea to an unknown region. Greek travelers and traders sailed on all the navigable rivers of Europe. In the 6th century BCE, they dealt with merchants who brought them tin from Cornwall in England along the rivers of France to the Greek port of Marseilles on the Mediterranean.

A scene from Homer's story of Jason's Search for the Golden Fleece. Greeks made many long journeys in their boats and were often away from home for years at a time.

Magna Graecia

Southern Italy, including the island of Sicily, was an important colony from the beginning. This area had the advantage of being close to the homeland, having natural harbors, rich farmland and local populations who were not hostile. Southern Italy had so many Greek colonists that it was known as Magna Graecia ("Greater Greece"). The Greeks had a profound influence on the local populations, including the Latins who would later replace them as the most powerful people in the ancient world.

When a city-state decided to set up a new colony it followed an established plan. First the city government selected a group of emigrants and appointed a leader. Then an oracle was consulted to confirm the choice of destination and leader, the best time to leave and other practical details. When the colonists left, they knew that they were leaving for good. In fact, Greek colonies were not considered in the way we consider modern colonies; although they stayed in touch with the homeland, they were independent from the start.

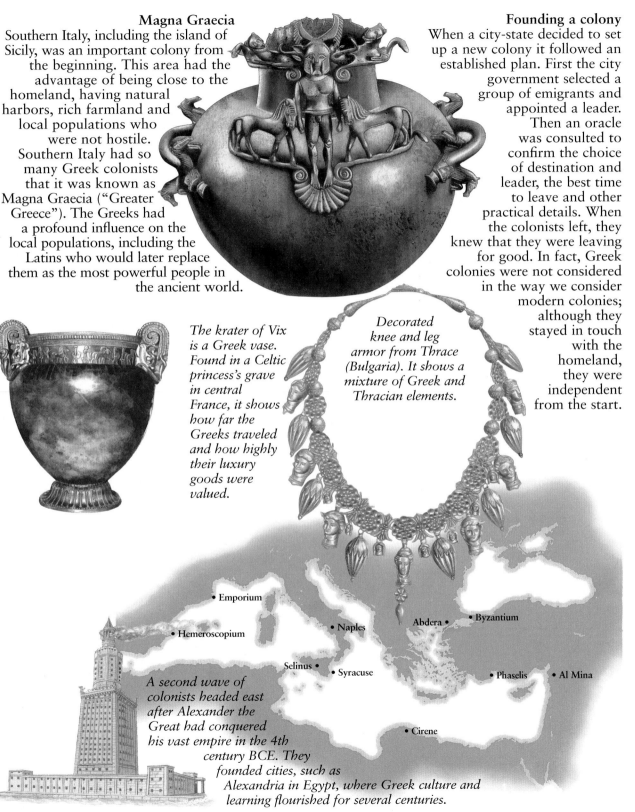

The krater of Vix is a Greek vase. Found in a Celtic princess's grave in central France, it shows how far the Greeks traveled and how highly their luxury goods were valued.

Decorated knee and leg armor from Thrace (Bulgaria). It shows a mixture of Greek and Thracian elements.

- Emporium
- Hemeroscopium
- Naples
- Abdera
- Byzantium
- Selinus
- Syracuse
- Phaselis
- Al Mina
- Cirene

A second wave of colonists headed east after Alexander the Great had conquered his vast empire in the 4th century BCE. They founded cities, such as Alexandria in Egypt, where Greek culture and learning flourished for several centuries.

GLOSSARY

acropolis "High city" in Greek. A central hill in a Greek city-state that was first used as a fortress and later for temples.

agora A marketplace; also, a meeting place for all inhabitants of a city-state.

amphora (plural: amphorae) Large, two-handled pottery jars used for storing wine and olive oil.

Archaic period The period of history in Greece that roughly spanned 750 BCE to 500 BCE, between the Dark Ages and Classical period.

banish To drive out or remove from a home or place.

cavalry Soldiers on horseback.

Chimera The fire-breathing female monster with a lion's head, goat's body and serpent's tail.

chiton Clothing made of two sheets of drapery that was worn over the body and usually tied with a belt around the waist.

city-state A small state that developed around a city or island in ancient Greece.

Classical period Historical period in Greece from about 500 to 336 BCE.

Delphi The place the Greeks believed to be the center of the world, and the home of the Oracle.

democracy A system of government in which all citizens have a vote.

epic poem A long story poem about heroic adventures and great battles.

fermenting Undergoing a controlled breakdown of a substance by enzymes, such as fermenting grape juice into wine.

Furies The goddesses of vengeance, who sprang from the blood of Uranos.

Gorgons In Greek mythology, the three sisters, Stheno, Euryale and Medusa, who had snakes for hair and who had the power to turn anyone who looked at them to stone.

Hellenistic period Historical period in Greece from about 336 to 147 BCE.

himation A type of garment usually draped over the left shoulder and around the body and used as a cloak.

hoplite A heavily armed Greek soldier.

krater A jar or vase that has a large round body and wide mouth and is used for mixing water and wine.

Labyrinth A complicated maze built by Daedalus in Crete.

lyre A stringed musical instrument similar to a small U-shaped harp.

Minotaur A mythical beast, half man, half bull, the offspring of Pasiphae and a bull. Daedalus confined the Minotaur in the Labyrinth.

mosaic A decoration made by setting small pieces of glass or stone of different colors on a surface to create pictures or patterns.

oracle A priestess through whom a god is believed to speak; an answer or decision given by such a person.

phalanx A battle formation of foot soldiers, or hoplites, in which the soldiers march side by side in a block.

pomegranate A reddish fruit about the size of an orange that has a thick skin and many edible seeds.

prophecy A prediction of the future.

sanctuary A sacred place or religious temple.

smelt To melt ores in order to get metals from them.

Titans Godlike giants, shaped like humans.

trident A three-pronged spear; a symbol of the sea god Poseidon.

trireme A Greek warship with three banks of oars.

votive statue A statue made in gratitude or devotion to a god.

FOR MORE INFORMATION

American School of Classical Studies in Athens
54 Souidias Street
GR-106 76 Athens
Greece
(+30) 210-72-36-313
Web site: http://www.ascsa.edu.gr
This organization provides students and scholars with a base for the advanced study of Greek culture—from antiquity to the present.

The Ancient Greek World
University of Pennsylvania Museum of Archaeology and Anthropology
3260 South Street
Philadelphia, PA 19104
(215) 898-4000
Web site: http://www.museum.upenn.edu/Greek_World/index.html
This Web site offers descriptions of the land, culture, daily life, religion and economy of the ancient Greek world.

History for Kids
Portland State University
Portland, OR 97207
Web site: http://www.historyforkids.org
Kidipede, or history for kids, provides information about human history, including Ancient Greece and mythology.

Metropolitan Museum of Art
Department of Greek and Roman Art
1000 Fifth Avenue
New York, NY 10028-0198
(212) 535-7710
Web site: http://www.metmuseum.org/Works_of_Art/greek_and_roman_art
The collection of Greek and Roman art at the Metropolitan Museum of Art, more than 17,000 works ranging in date from the Neolithic period to the time of the Roman emperor Constantine's conversion to Christianity in 312 CE, includes the art of many cultures and is among the most comprehensive in North America.

National Junior Classical League
422 Wells Mill Drive
Miami University
Oxford, OH 45056-1694
(513) 529-7741
Web site: http://www.njcl.org
This organization of junior and senior high school students is sponsored by the American Classical League. It

encourages an interest in and appreciation of the language, art, literature and culture of ancient Greece and Rome.

The Perseus Digital Library
Tufts University
Medford, MA 02155
Web site: http://www.perseus.tufts.edu
This digital library provides information on the humanities and offers collections on history, literature and culture of the Greco-Roman world.

Web Sites

Due to the changing nature of Internet links, Rosen Publishing has developed an online list of Web sites related to the subject of this book. The site is updated regularly. Please use this link to access the list:

http://www.rosenlinks.com/anc/gree

FOR FURTHER READING

Adkins, Lesley, and Roy A. Adkins. *Handbook to Life in Ancient Greece*. New York, NY: Facts On File, 2005.

Bargallo, Eva. *Greece* (Ancient Civilizations). New York, NY: Chelsea House, 2005.

Bolton, Leslie. *The Everything Classical Mythology Book: Greek and Roman Gods, Goddesses, Heroes, and Monsters from Ares to Zeus*. Avon, MA: Adams Media Corporation, 2002.

Chisholm, Jane. *Encyclopedia of Ancient Greece*. Eveleth, MN: Usborne Books, 2007.

Coolidge, Olivia. *Greek Myths*. Boston, MA: Houghton Mifflin Company, 2001.

Daly, Kathleen N. *Greek and Roman Mythology A to Z*. Revised by Marian Rengel. 9 volumes. New York, NY: Chelsea House, 2003.

Durando, Furio. *Ancient Greece: The Dawn of the Western World*. New York, NY: Barnes and Noble Books, 2004.

Maynard, Charles W. *The Technology of Ancient Greece* (The Technology of the Ancient World). New York, NY: Rosen Publishing, 2006.

Nardo, Don. *Heroes: Discovering Mythology*. San Diego, CA: Lucent Books, 2002.

Nardo, Don. *Living in Ancient Greece*. San Diego, CA: Greenhaven Press, 2004.

Payment, Simone. *Greek Mythology* (Mythology Around the World). New York, NY: Rosen Publishing, 2006.

Powell, Anton. *Ancient Greece* (Cultural Atlas for Young People). New York, NY: Chelsea House Publishers, 2007.

Roberts, Russell. *Zeus* (Profiles in Greek and Roman Mythology). Hockessin, DE: Mitchell Lane Publishers, 2007.

Warner, Rex. *Men and Gods: Myths and Legends of the Ancient Greeks*. New York, NY: NYRB Classics, 2008.

INDEX

A

acropolis, 13, 15, 16, 17
Aegisthus, 10
Aeschylus, 24
Agamemnon, 10, 27
Alexander the Great, 28, 29, 43
Alexandria, 43
All-Athens Festival, 12
alphabets, 8, 9, 32
Anatolia, 5, 40
Aphrodite, 7, 12
Apollo, 10, 12
   Oracle of, 13
Arachne, 18
archaeologists, 8, 41, 42
Archaic period, 8, 9, 21, 25, 28
Aristarchus of Samos, 32
Aristophanes, 24
Aristotle, 33
Artemis, 12
astronomy, 5, 32
Athena, 12, 13, 15, 16, 18, 38
Athens, 13, 15, 16, 24, 28, 30,
   40, 41

B

Bellerophon, 38
Black Sea, 5, 42
Bulgaria *see* Thrace

C

Carthaginians, 42
Cassandra, 10, 27
Chimera, 38
City Dionysia, 12
city-states, 5, 9, 12, 16, 17, 28,
   29, 40, 41, 42
Classical period, 8, 9, 16, 24
clothes, 20, 21
Clytemnestra, 10
coins, 8, 21, 36, 40

colonies, 5, 9, 13, 40, 41 42, 43
Copernicus, 32
Corinth, 29
Cornwall, 42
crafts, 13, 17, 41
Crete, 8, 25, 30
Cronos, 7
Cycladic Islands, 8
Cyclopes, 7

D

Daedalus, 30
Danae, 38
Darius, King, 29
"Dark Ages," 9
Demeter, 7, 12, 34, 36
Dionysos, 9, 12, 22, 23, 40

E

education, 32
Egypt, 43
Elba, 42
England, 42
Etruscans, 42
Euripides, 24

F

farming, 12, 17, 28, 36, 37, 41
France, 42, 43
Furies, 7

G

Gaia, 7
Ganymede, 9
government, 8, 9, 16, 17, 43

H

Hades, 7, 34, 38
Hecuba, 10
Helen, 10, 27
Hephaestos, 15

Hera, 7, 22
Hermes, 12, 34
Hero of Alexandria, 33
Hestia, 7, 12
Homer, 5, 25, 28, 42
Hippocrates, 33

I

Icarus, 30
Iliad, 5, 25, 28
India, 28, 29
Issus, Battle of, 29
Italy, 42, 43

K

Knossos, 8

L

Labyrinth, 30
Latins, 43
Linear A script, 8
Linear B script, 8

M

Macedonia, 29
Magna Graecia, 43
Marseilles, 42
mathematics, 5, 32, 33
medicine, 5, 33
Mediterranean region, 5, 8, 9,
   41, 42
Mediterranean Sea, 8, 40, 42
Medusa, 38
Menander, 24
Menelaus, King, 10, 27
Metis, 15
Minoan civilization, 8
Minos, King, 8, 30
Minotaur, 30
Mycenae, 8, 10, 28
Mycenaean script, 32

N

Naples, 42
North Africa, 41
Nymphs, 7

O

Odysseus, 20, 27
Odyssey, 5, 24, 25
olives, 12, 15, 36, 37, 40, 41
Olympic Games, 9, 24
Olympus, Mount, 7, 9, 12, 38
Oracles, 12, 13, 43

P

Panathenaia, 12
Paris, 10, 27
Parthenon, 13
Pasiphae, 30
Pegasus, 38
Peloponnesian Wars, 28
Penelope, 20
Pericles, 16
Persephone, 34
Perseus, 38
Persian Empire, 28
philosophy, 5, 8, 9, 33
Phoenicians, 9

Piraeus, 41
Plato, 33
poets/poetry, 5, 25, 32
Poseidon, 7, 12, 15, 30, 38
Priam, King of Troy, 10
Pythagoras, 32

R

religion, 12, 13
Renaissance, 5
Rhea, 7
Romans, 5, 12, 29
Russia, 40, 42

S

Satyrs, 23
science, 9, 32, 33
Semele, 22
ships, 17, 23, 27, 29, 40, 41, 42
Sicily, 30
Silenus, 9, 22
slaves, 17, 23, 24, 25, 40
Socrates, 33
soldiers, 28, 29
Sophocles, 24
Sparta, 16, 24, 27, 28, 29
sport, 24

T

Thales of Miletus, 33
theater, 8, 22, 24, 25
Thrace, 43
Titanesses, 7, 15
Titans, 7
trade, 40, 41, 42
Trojans, 10, 27
Troy, 10, 27, 28
Turkey, 5, 40

U

Underworld, 7, 12, 34

W

war, 12, 13, 18, 20, 27, 28, 29
weaving, 18, 20
Western culture, 5, 8, 32, 33
wool, 18, 20, 40
women, 13, 17, 20, 21, 24, 25, 32

Z

Zeus, 5, 7, 9, 12, 15, 22, 34, 38